For a Grieving Heart

Terri Ann Leidich

Photography by
Glenn Leidich and Bill Hollinshead

A Gift for a Heart
That is Grieving

I do not know what you are going through . . . none of us can really know unless we walk in your shoes. But I care and I want to care in a way that supports you and acknowledges your pain and struggle. My hope is that this book will help put words to your emotions, give feelings to your confusion, and lend hope at a time that must feel hopeless.

To: _____

From: _____

Date: _____

For a Grieving Heart

Published in the United States by BQB Publishing

(Boutqiue of Quality Books Publishing)

www.bqbpublishing.com

Printed in the United States of America

ISBN 978-0-9828689-4-2 (h)
ISBN 978-1-937084-86-8 (p)
ISBN 978-0-9831699-5-6 (e)

Library of Congress No. 2010934526

Book cover design
by Darlene Swanson
www.van-garde.com

Book interior design
by Robin Krauss
www.lindendesign.biz

In grateful acknowledgment to my dear friend,
Katie Hollinshead, for helping me understand
that the poetry I wrote during my intense time of grief
has a purpose and a message all its own.

A special thank you to
my husband, Glenn Leidich,
and my friend, Bill Hollinshead,
for the beautiful photography
that speaks right to our hearts.

From My Heart to Yours

None of us asks for grief, yet every one of us will at some time in our lives feel its sharp fangs and suffer from the aftermath of its attack. When my son was killed in an accident at the age of 20, my world as I knew it collapsed and I was thrown into a black hole of grief that felt like it would devour me. Because writing is a passion and a refuge, I wrote . . . and the poetry in this book is a result of some of that writing.

While the poems in this book are about the loss of a child, a son, grief is universal in that its many twists, turns, and emotions are similar whether you've lost a child, a parent, a spouse, or a friend. To help you in your grief, personalize the verses I've written to reflect your loss and your pain, to express your agony or your confusion. Use these words in ways that work for you.

When I was caught in the darkness of grief, I just wanted to know that someone understood because it often felt as though no one seemed to grasp the life-changing, enduring pain that I was going through. I also wanted to be assured that I would survive the experience because I was often convinced that I would not make it through the agony. And I wanted someone to hold on to me during those times that I wasn't sure I wanted to continue on.

My hope is that the words in these poems will help you to know that I do understand and that you will survive. You will change, and that process in itself is painful, but you will endure and eventually move on to fully live life again. Give yourself the time to do that. Love yourself through the process and hold firmly to the love that you have for the one who has moved on from this earth. Let that love be a blanket of warmth during this winter of your life.

Please know that my heart is with you even though we have never met . . . because those of us who have lost someone precious to us are bonded on a level beyond our understanding. It is at that level that I meet you, I understand your agony, and I support you in your journey.

Terri Ann Leidich

4

I know my son is in heaven, Lord.
I know my child is with you.
I know you are caring for him, Lord,
but what is a mother to do?

My arms reach out to hold him.
My hands long to touch him once more.
My eyes just long to see him.
My heart is constantly sore.

My life is so lonesome without him.
My dreams are no longer there.
My plans have withered and dried,
but my soul still longs to share.

I know you loaned him to me, Lord
my tiny son so sweet.
To feed, to clothe, to guide, to love
until you called him home above.
But Lord so soon?

I question you.
I had him but a while . . .
this son so precious and so dear,
my own sweet youngest child.

I was prepared to say goodbye
as he went out the door.
But I really wasn't ready, Lord
that it be forevermore.

Moment by moment
Dear Lord I pray,
Give me the strength
To face each day.

Weakened and grieving
Sunk in despair,
I desperately need to
Feel that you care.

Feelings whirl
and twirl in
a hollow heart.

Empty, alone,
confused.

Searching, pulling,
seeking a greater being,
a higher power,
an answer.

Gentle angel up above
looking down at me
with love.

Cradle me with
loving care
assuring me
you're really there.

Let me feel
your gentle smile
and stay with me
for just a while,

As I adjust to you
up there.
My special angel
in heavenly air.

Deep inside of me
resides a soul.
An empty, hollow soul.
A shell of what I could be,
unseeing of what I am.

A turning, churning soul
swallowed by aloneness
and fear.

A grasping, clinging,
unyielding soul,
waiting to be heard,
filled with pain,
faith, and belief.

Silent angel, hovering over me,
gently placing kisses on my cheeks.

You are such a part of my life now,
how can I grieve that you are gone?

I don't have you in physical form,
I can't feel the strength of your hugs.

But I still feel the gentleness
of your caring and I hear the ring of your
laughter.

I no longer hear your voice with my ears,
I hear it through my heart and soul.

Silent angel hovering over me,
you continue to touch my life.

We've changed roles, you and I.
I was the one who guided you.

Now you lead me by the hand
softly whispering through my mind,

Thoughts and ideas
that are more like you than me.

God, please hold my son,
since I can't.

Assure him that he is special,
since I can't.

Give him all he needs to grow
and guide him on his way,
since I can't.

And when he does something wonderful,
let him know it,
since I can't.

Enjoy him, Lord,
every special thing about him,
since I can't.

And hold him safe in heaven's arms
until I get there,
so I can.

He was one of my reasons for living;
the brightest of all twinkling stars.
I clung to all he was
the way moisture sits
gently on a morning leaf.

My heart cries out and rebels
at his never living again.
Unfairness ignites my anger
like a match ignites a
pile of dried pine needles.

Hopelessness envelopes my spirit
and carries it to the
bitter depths of hell
leaving only a broken, empty shell.

I cannot think of tomorrow
when all my yesterdays
have been gathered together
and smashed like a helpless ship
by angry ocean waves
against razor-edged rocks.

Oh grief,
you many tentacled monster
standing in the middle of my world,
pulling me toward
the open pit of darkness.

Confusing me with your many arms
of anger, sorrow, guilt, and pain.
Ever, ever pulling me toward the darkness
as if no light will ever shine
in my world again.

Hideous monster,
how did I not know the forcefulness
of your existence
until you wrapped your vicious arms
around me and squeezed my life
from my very soul?

Doubt . . .
oh dark, circling emotion,
pulling me down, down
drowning me in fear and pain.

Doubt . . .
dark, hopeless feeling,
painful, aching feeling,
circling, circling around me.

Pulling . . .
pulling me down
into your dreary depths.

Gentle angel sleeping nigh,
can you hear my painful sigh,
of loneliness and dreams forsaken,
a future of hope badly shaken,
by the empty cavern in my heart,
where you were once a living part?

Gentle spirit hovering above
touch me sweetly
with your soul
and place a gentle kiss
on my heart.

Son, oh my son,
I miss you.
I'll always miss you.
Life, days, years
will never take that away.

I once had a son who wore his cap like that.
The brim to the back and the thin plastic
adjusting band
on his forehead, over his fine, blond hair.

A son whose intense blue eyes
spoke of the dreams, ideas, and plans
that jogged around in his mind.

A son whose future was bright because of
his intelligence, his ambition, and his ability
to love without judgment.

I once had a son who wore his cap like that.

A son who loved motorcycles and wanted one of
his own.
We wouldn't give in. I'm good on
a motorcycle, Mom, he'd plead.
It's the other guy you have to watch
out for, his father would warn.

I once had a son who wore his cap like that.

He'd often borrow motorcycles from
his friends and go for rides.
It helps me clear my mind, he'd say.

One day while he was clearing his mind,
a car pulled out in front of him.

I once had a son who wore his cap like that.

Lord, do you hear me?
Do you really care?
I used to believe you did,
But now . . .
Now, I'm infected with doubt.

Could you love me
And take my son?
Could you have my
Best interest in mind
And let him die?

I don't know.
I don't understand.
Maybe I'm not supposed to.
And that's the biggest
Confusion of all.

Life, oh meaningless
rolling of endless days,
why do you continue?

What is left
in your depth of years
that can bring me any joy?

Sing to me of dreams . . . my dreams.
What dreams?
Dreams that long ago died or never were.

Which?
I know not.
Dreaming seems so foreign to me.
I don't know if I ever experienced it.

Perhaps once . . .
before the pain . . .
before the death of my son.

But dream now,
my soul encourages.

Why?
I scream in return.

Why should I dream
only to have those dreams
trampled before my very eyes
as heavenly laughter echoes
through the skies.

I can't take that pain . . .
not again.
But what choice have I?
To never dream again?
To never try?

That's not much of a choice.
Not much of a life.

Trees move gently
to the rhythm
of the wind.

As my mind moves softly
to the beating
of my heart.

Keep your beating gentle
oh my heart,
so my mind won't race,

In a frantic, frenzied chase
for answers and reasons
that my gentle, beating heart
already knows.

Once upon this present time
a mother mourns for her son.

Her tears fall in abundance
upon the mound of grass beneath which he lies.

Each tear penetrates deep within the ground,
giving the soil enrichment.

From far above
a son smiles down upon his mother.

He still feels the tenderness of her love.
The memories of all she had brought
to his life on earth bring tender tears
to his heavenly eyes.

The tears roll down from the heavens
in huge thunderous clouds;
they permeate the soil
and join the tears of his mother.

The love of mother and son
unites deep within the ground
where moisture spreads out its hands
and feeds the soil which
nurtures the beauty of nature.

The grass grows, the flowers bloom,
and life goes on because of a mother's love.